From Your Friends At The MAILBOX®

W9-BJP-647

Busy Kids™

SNACKTIME

Written by:
Jan Brennan
Lisa Leonardi
Dayle Timmons

Edited by:
Jayne M. Gammons
Ada Goren

Illustrated by:
Susan Hodnett
Rebecca Saunders

Cover designed by:
Kimberly Richard

www.themailbox.com

©1998 by THE EDUCATION CENTER, INC.
All rights reserved.

ISBN #1-56234-237-1

Except as provided herein, no part of this publication may be reproduced or transmitted in any form or by any means, electronic or mechanical, including photocopying, recording, or storing in any information storage and retrieval system or electronic online bulletin board, without prior written permission from The Education Center, Inc. Permission is given to the original purchaser to reproduce patterns and reproducibles for individual classroom use only and not for resale or distribution. Reproduction for an entire school or school system is prohibited. Please direct written inquiries to The Education Center, Inc., P.O. Box 9753, Greensboro, NC 27429-0753. The Education Center®, The Mailbox®, Busy Kids™, and the mailbox/post/grass logo are trademarks of The Education Center, Inc., and may be the subject of one or more federal trademark registrations. All other brand or product names are trademarks or registered trademarks of their respective companies.

Manufactured in the United States
10 9 8 7 6 5 4 3 2

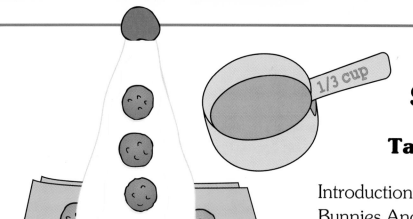

Busy Kids™
Snacktime

Table Of Contents

Introduction

Look through the pages of *Busy Kids™: Snacktime* to find 30 clever recipes based on some of early childhood's most popular themes. The step-by-step format is designed so that individuals or small groups of youngsters can follow each recipe from start to finish with little or no help from the teacher. What a fun way to build youngsters' self-confidence! And you'll be mixing important skills into your snacktime as youngsters develop their small-muscle coordination and work on measurement, counting, language skills, and much more. Happy snacking to you and your little chefs!

Tips For The Chief Cook

Ingredients:
Plan ahead and make a weekly run to the supermarket. Or ask parents to help by making food donations.

Utensils And Supplies:
At the beginning of the school year, ask parents to help you stock up on disposable items, such as paper plates, napkins, and plastic utensils. Create a treasure chest of handy utensils, such as a sharp knife (for teacher use), cookie cutters, measuring spoons and cups, a cutting board, and plastic bowls.

Teacher Preparation:
A few recipes require the use of an electrical appliance before the kids start cooking. Consider keeping a toaster oven or electric frying pan in your classroom—or develop a good relationship with the school cook!

Step-By-Step Directions:
If desired, remove the step-by-step direction cards from this book. (The recipes are printed back-to-back for this purpose.) You may choose to leave each page as is, or cut it into six individual cards. Either way, you'll probably want to laminate each recipe, then display it in your cooking area so your youngsters can easily see and follow the visual directions.

What To Do When The Snack Is Through

Don't want to waste leftover ingredients? Check out the creative idea following each recipe for a way to use extra ingredients to enhance learning.

BUNNIES AND BASKETS

BUNNY CAKE

Ingredients:
1 cupcake per child
white frosting
jelly beans
minimarshmallows
string licorice
1 Keebler® Cookie Stix™ cookie (or other stick-shaped cookie) per child

Utensils And Supplies:
1 plastic knife (or craft stick) per child
napkins

Teacher Preparation:
   Prepare a class supply of cupcakes in paper baking cups. Cut six 1 1/2-inch lengths of string licorice for each child. Cut one Keebler® Cookie Stix™ in half per child. Arrange the ingredients and utensils near the step-by-step direction cards.

WHAT TO DO WHEN THE SNACK IS THROUGH

   Can your little bunnies identify a jelly bean by using only their sense of taste? Try this simple jelly-bean taste test to find out. Display one jelly bean of each color in front of the class. Direct a student volunteer to close his eyes. Place a leftover jelly bean in his hand and have him keep his eyes closed while he eats it. Then ask him to view the jelly-bean lineup and point to the color he tasted. Invite your entire bunch of bunnies to put their taste buds to this test.

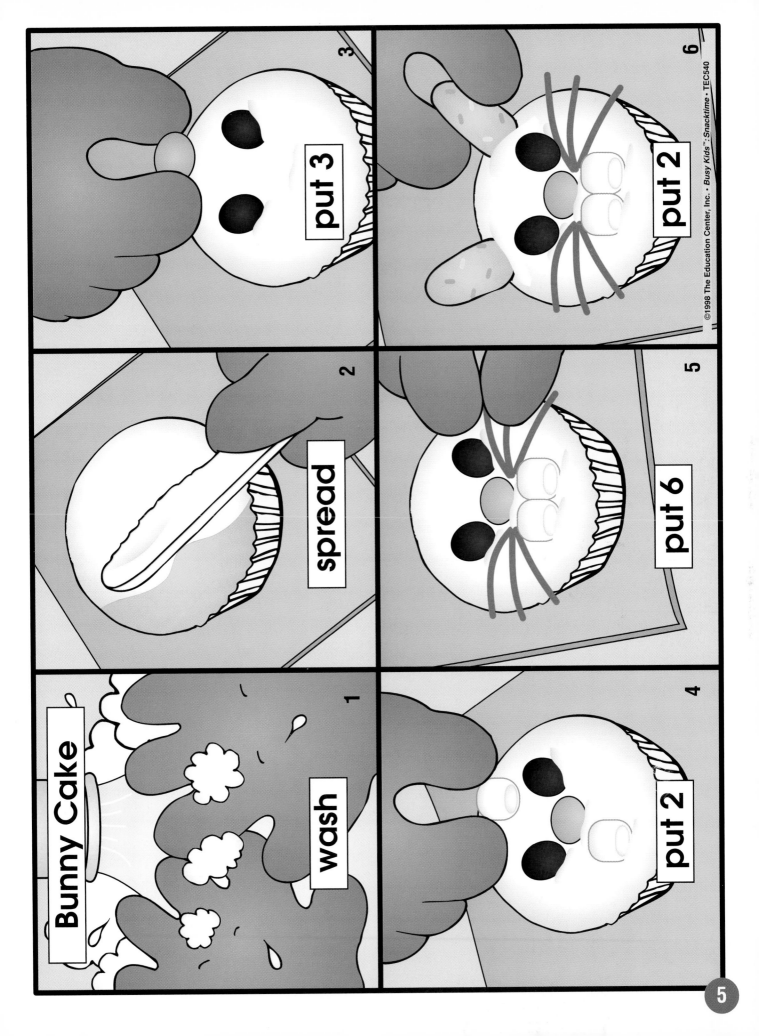

Bunny Cake

wash 1

spread 2

put 3 3

put 2 4

put 6 5

put 2 6

©1998 The Education Center, Inc. • Busy Kids™ •Snacktime • TEC540

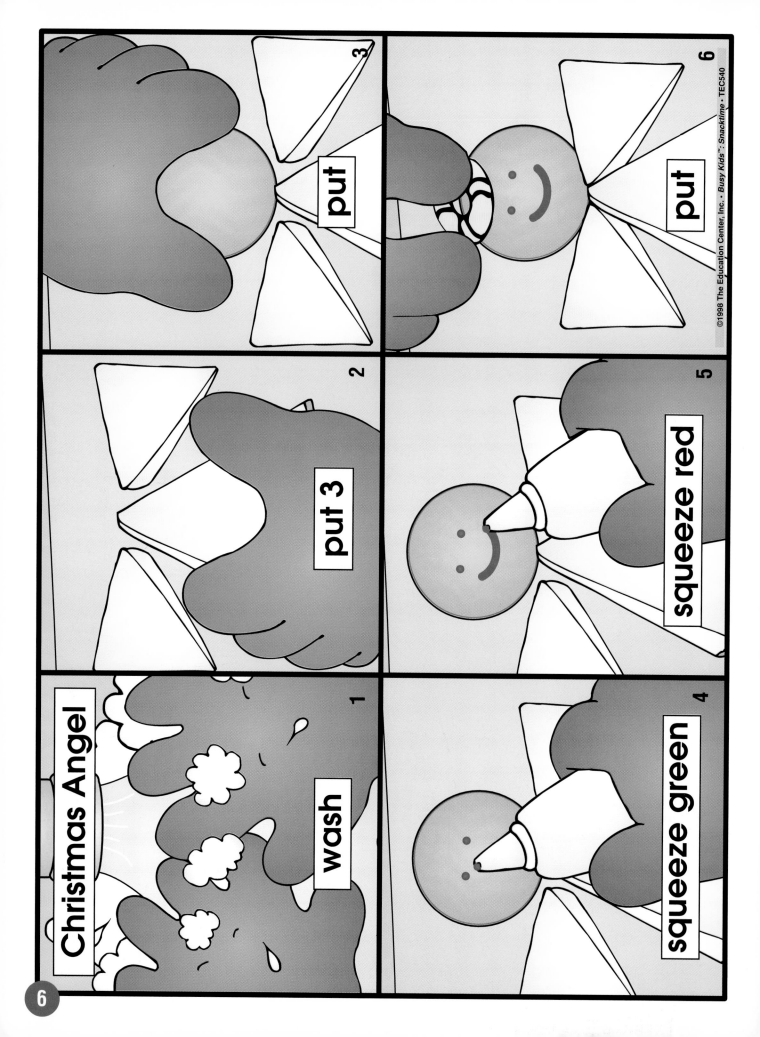

Christmas Angel

wash

put 3

put

squeeze green

squeeze red

put

©1998 The Education Center, Inc. • Busy Kids™: Snacktime • TEC540

6

Christmas

Christmas Angel

Ingredients:
1 slice of angel food cake per child
1 vanilla wafer per child
tubes of red and green decorating icing
1 Gummi Savers® candy per child

Utensils And Supplies:
knife
napkins

Teacher Preparation:
   Cut each slice of angel food cake in half diagonally. Then cut one of the halves on the diagonal again, to give each child a total of three triangles. Arrange the ingredients and utensils near the step-by-step direction cards.

What To Do When The Snack Is Through

   After youngsters make a yummy Christmas snack for themselves, invite them to make one for their feathered friends. Give each child two leftover vanilla wafers, peanut butter, and a pipe cleaner. Instruct each child to spread peanut butter on the bottoms of both cookies, then stick them together. Help him loop the pipe cleaner around the cookies and twist the ends together. Have him bend the twisted pipe cleaner into a hook shape. Have him spread more peanut butter over the outside of his cookie ornament, then dip it in birdseed. Hang the finished cookie ornaments on a tree for the birds to eat.

CIRCUS

Clown Hat

Ingredients:
1 sugar cone per child
white frosting
round, berry-flavored cereal (such as Cap'n Crunch's
   Oops! All Berries™)
1 red maraschino cherry per child

Utensils And Supplies:
1 plastic knife (or craft stick) per child
spoon
napkins

Teacher Preparation:
   Drain the cherries; then remove the stems.
Arrange the ingredients and utensils near the step-
by-step direction cards.

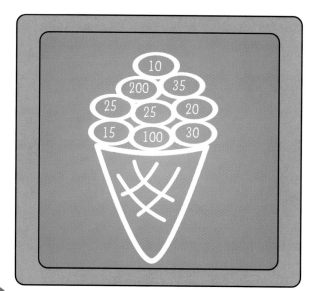

What To Do When The Snack Is Through

   Challenge your little ones to estimate the number of leftover berry cereal pieces it will take to fill an ice-cream cone. If desired, draw an ice-cream cone on the chalkboard. Write each child's estimate in a circle above the cone. Then have youngsters count along as you fill the real cone with one piece of cereal at a time. Discuss which estimates were closest to the actual number.

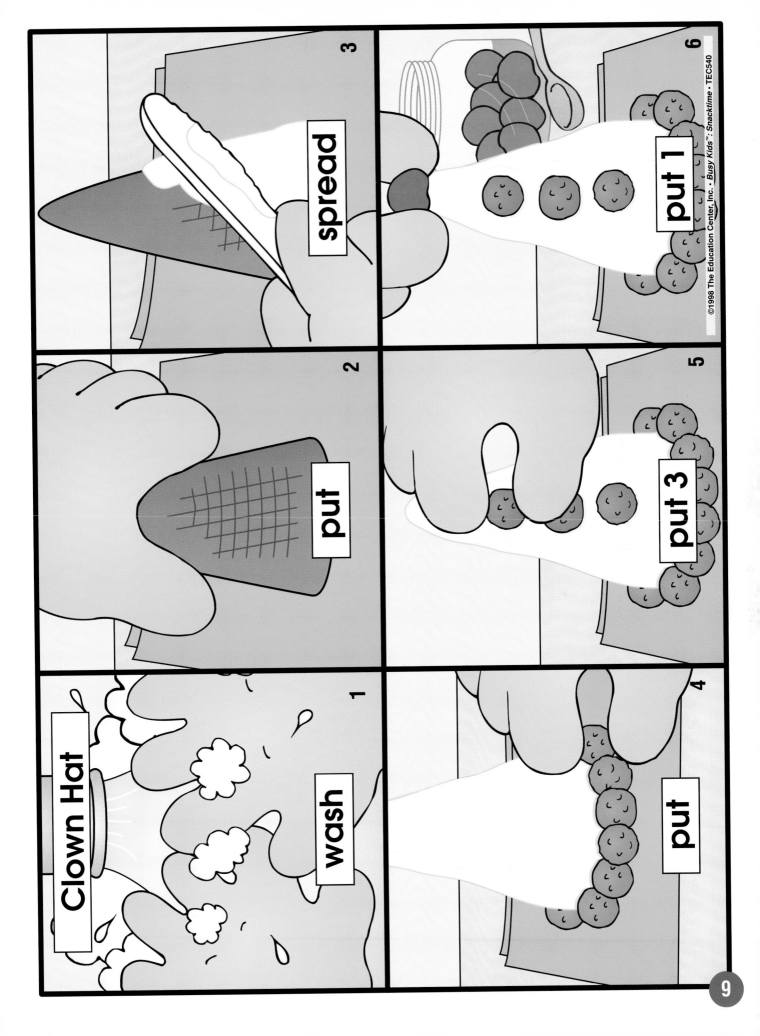

Clown Hat

wash **1**

put **2**

spread **3**

put **4**

put 3 **5**

put 1 **6**

©1998 The Education Center, Inc. • *Busy Kids*™: *Snacktime* • TEC540

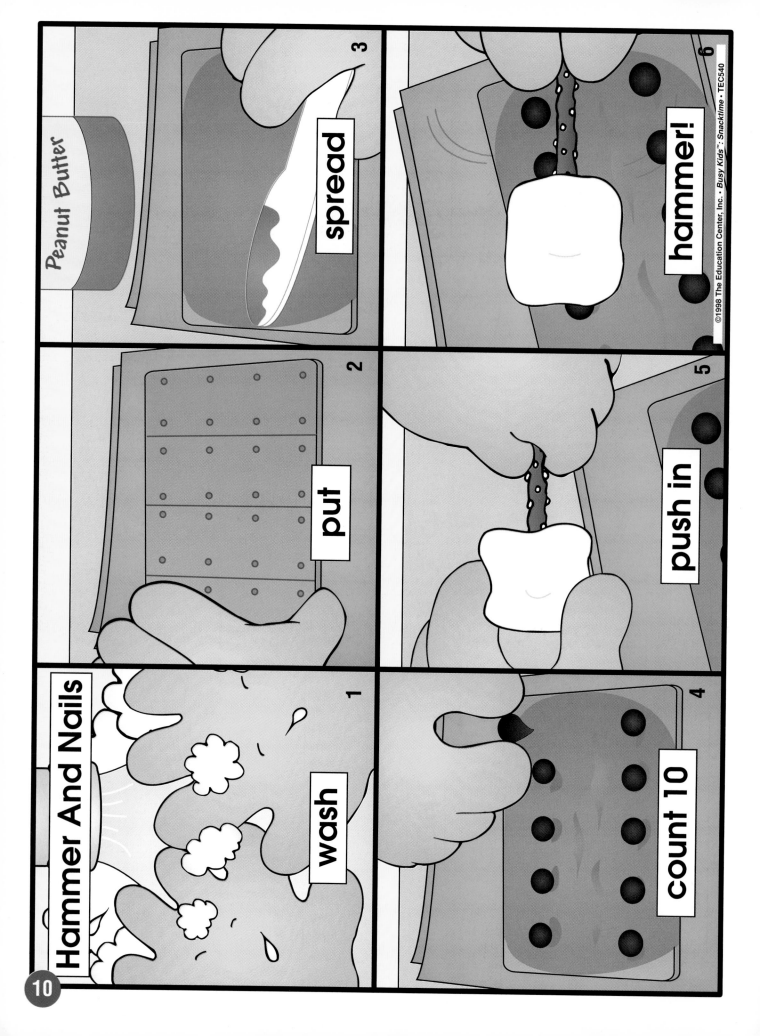

©1998 The Education Center, Inc. • Busy Kids™: Snacktime • TEC540

Community Helpers

Hammer And Nails

Ingredients:
1 graham cracker per child
peanut butter
1 large marshmallow per child
1 pretzel stick per child
chocolate chips

Utensils And Supplies:
1 plastic knife (or craft stick) per child
napkins

Teacher Preparation:
   Arrange the ingredients and utensils near the step-by-step direction cards.

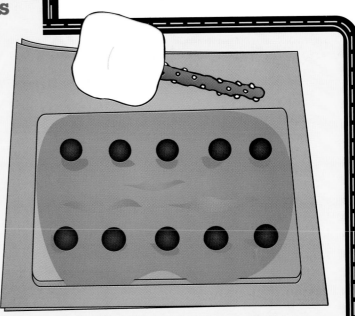

What To Do When The Snack Is Through
Explain to youngsters that ants live together in a community, with each ant having a job to do to help its community. Many ants have the job of gathering food, and your little ones can watch these workers in action! Search your school or center grounds for an anthill; then place a large plastic hoop around it. Along the inside of the hoop, spread a few leftover pretzels, marshmallows, and chocolate chips. Have students stand around the hoop. Caution youngsters not to touch the food or the ants. Stand back and observe the ants go marching one by one to work!

Dinosaurs

Dino Land

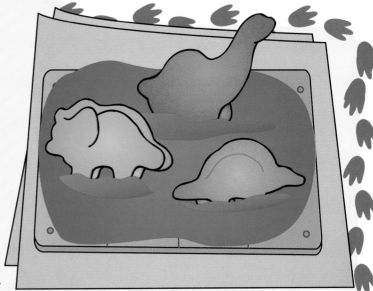

Ingredients:
1 graham cracker per child
soft cream cheese
green food coloring
3 Gummy dinosaurs per child

Utensils And Supplies:
1 plastic knife (or craft stick) per child
napkins
spoon

Teacher Preparation:
Tint cream cheese with green food coloring.
Arrange the ingredients and utensils near the step-
by-step direction cards.

What To Do When The Snack Is Through

Count on dinosaurs for some "tremenda-saurus"
sorting practice! Encourage your little dinosaur lovers
to sort the leftover Gummy dinosaurs by color and
then by type. Have youngsters count the number of
dinosaurs in each group. Can your students name the
group with the most dinosaurs? The fewest dinosaurs?
There's much fun in store with "dino-sorts"!

©1998 The Education Center, Inc. • *Busy Kids*™ • *Snacktime* • TEC540

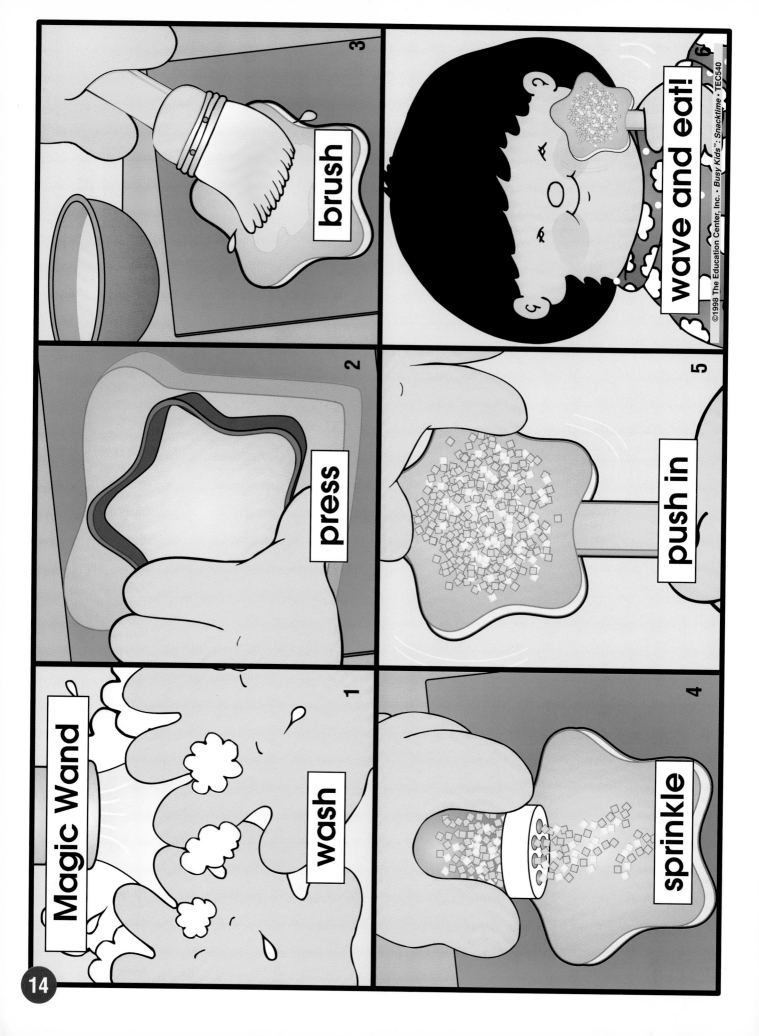

©1998 The Education Center, Inc. • Busy Kids™: Snacktime • TEC540

Fairy Tales

Magic Wand

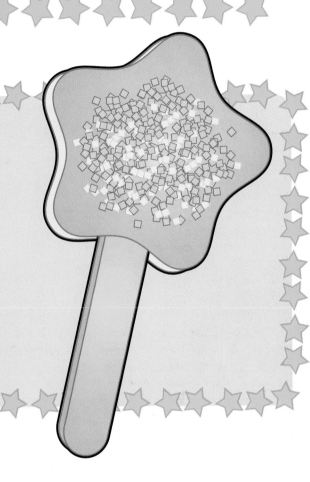

Ingredients:
1 slice of toast per child
melted butter
blue sugar sprinkles

Utensils And Supplies:
1 jumbo craft stick per child
napkins
star-shaped cookie cutter
pastry brush

Teacher Preparation:
   Toast a slice of bread for each child. Melt the butter. Arrange the ingredients and utensils near the step-by-step direction cards.

Dear boys and girls,

Here's some candy for you from my house. Hansel and Gretel enjoyed it, and I know you will, too!

Your friend,
Wanda Witch

What To Do When The Snack Is Through

   Don't toss those toast scraps! Use them for acting out a fun twist to the story of *Hansel And Gretel.* Tear the toast scraps into small pieces. Before school one day, make a winding trail of bread crumbs outdoors, leading from your classroom (or building) to another location at your school or center. Leave a box of wrapped candy at the end of the trail, along with the note shown. When youngsters arrive, point out the bread-crumb trail and invite them to follow it. Surprise!

15

Fall Harvest

Potato Pal

Ingredients:
1 baked potato per child
string beans
broccoli flowerets
baby carrots
raisins
red peppers
butter (optional)

Utensils And Supplies:
1 paper plate per child
plastic forks
knife

Teacher Preparation:
Bake one potato for each child; then cool.
Wash all of the vegetables. Separate the broccoli
flowerets, slice the peppers, and cut the carrots in
half. Arrange the ingredients and utensils near the
step-by-step direction cards. If desired, have butter
available for children who wish to add it to
their baked potatoes when it is time to
eat the snack.

What To Do When The Snack Is Through

Harvest some fall fun with this printing project.
Draw a large cornucopia shape on bulletin-board paper. Lay it on the art table next to the following supplies: several shallow containers of tempera paints in
autumn colors, raw potato halves, and other vegetables left over from the recipe. Invite your children
to dip the various vegetables into the paints and then
make prints of the vegetables directly on the cornucopia. When the paint is dry, display this collaborative
cornucopia for all to see!

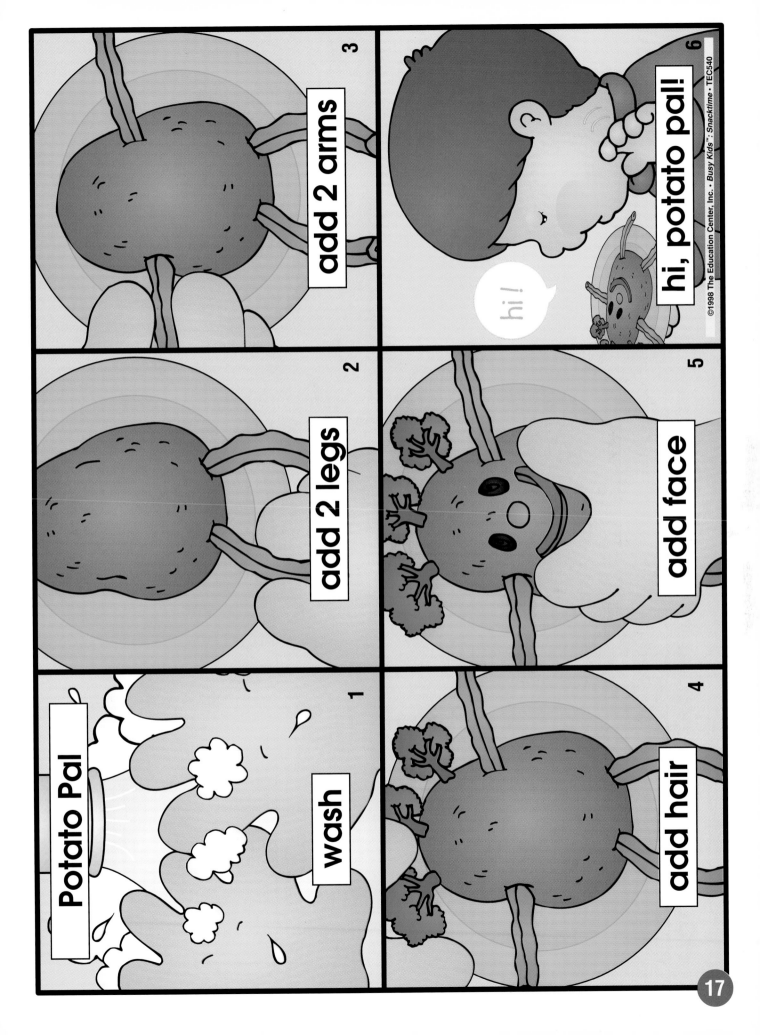

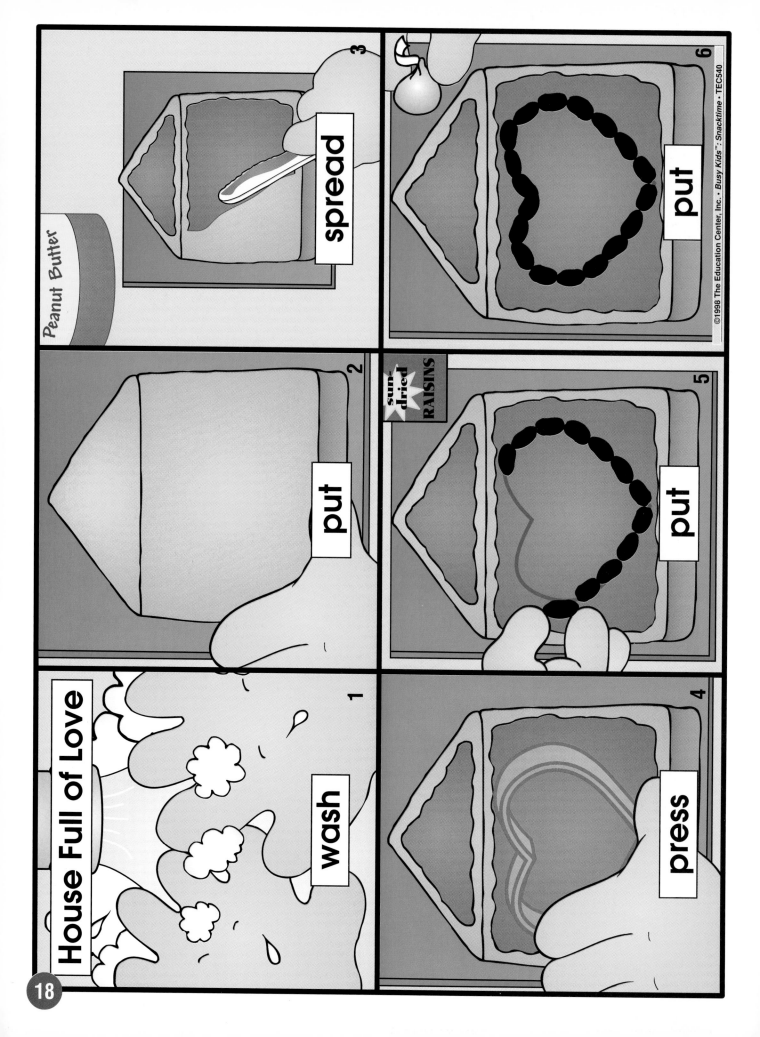

Family

House Full of Love

Ingredients:
1 1/2 slices of bread per child
peanut butter
raisins
1 Hershey's® Kiss® per child

Utensils And Supplies:
1 plastic knife (or craft stick) per child
heart-shaped cookie cutter
napkins
knife

Teacher Preparation:
Remove the crust from each slice of bread. Cut the necessary number of bread slices in half (diagonally). Arrange the ingredients and utensils near the step-by-step direction cards.

What To Do When The Snack Is Through

You're bound to have sweet success with this activity that provides practice with patterning and ordinal numbers. Distribute an equal number of the leftover Hershey's® Kisses® and raisins. Have your own supply handy. Create a pattern, such as *candy, raisin, candy, raisin.* Have youngsters copy or extend your pattern, or encourage them to create their own patterns. Then have each youngster unwrap his candies and put them in a row. Have him line up his raisins separately. Give directions using ordinal numbers, such as, "Eat your third raisin," or "Eat your second Hershey's® Kiss®." Vary the ordinal number and the food item until *every* morsel is eaten!

The Farm

Top Slops

Ingredients:
1/3 cup applesauce per child
1 tablespoon raisins per child
1 tablespoon chopped dried apple per child
1 tablespoon grated carrot per child

Utensils And Supplies:
1 five-ounce paper cup per child
1 plastic spoon per child
1/3 cup measuring cup
1 tablespoon

Teacher Preparation:
   Chop the necessary number of dried apple rings. Wash, peel, and grate the necessary number of carrots. Arrange the ingredients and utensils near the step-by-step direction cards.

There's no juice in a raisin!

What To Do When The Snack Is Through
   What makes dried fruit different from fresh fruit? Help little ones find out with this science experiment. Set out some fresh grapes and some leftover raisins. Ask a small group of youngsters to examine the foods carefully. Explain that the raisins used to be grapes. Invite the children to offer explanations for how the grapes became raisins. Then use a sharp knife to cut into a few grapes and a few raisins. Ask youngsters to examine the fruit again. What do they see in the grapes that is missing from the raisins? What a juicy discovery!

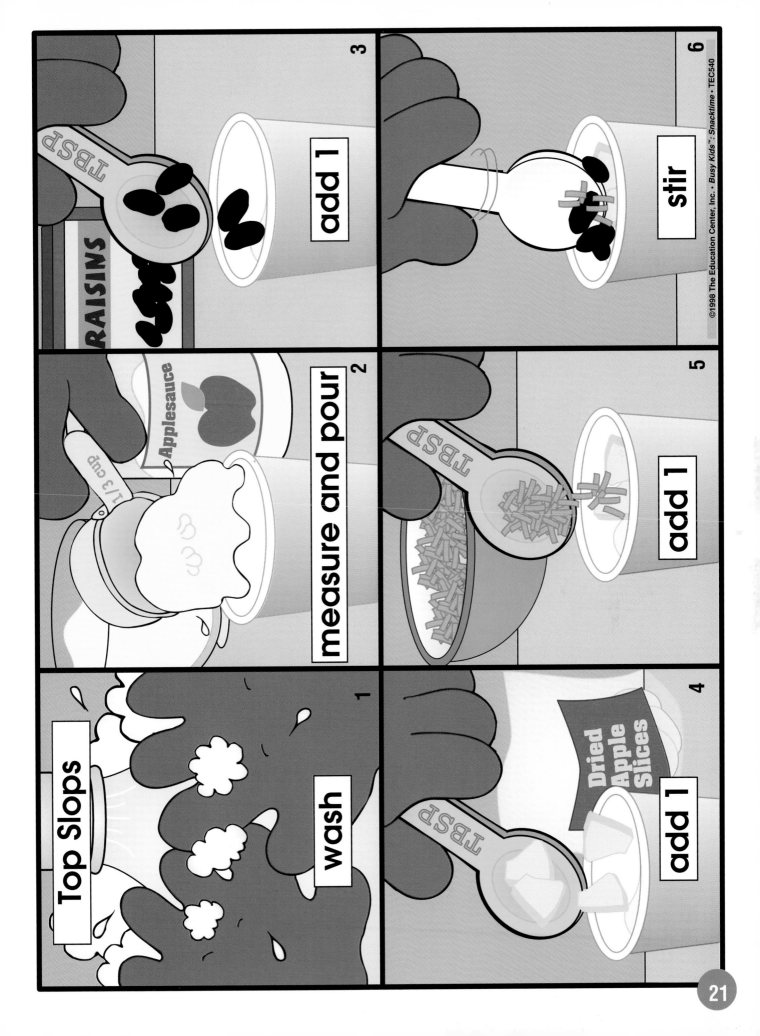

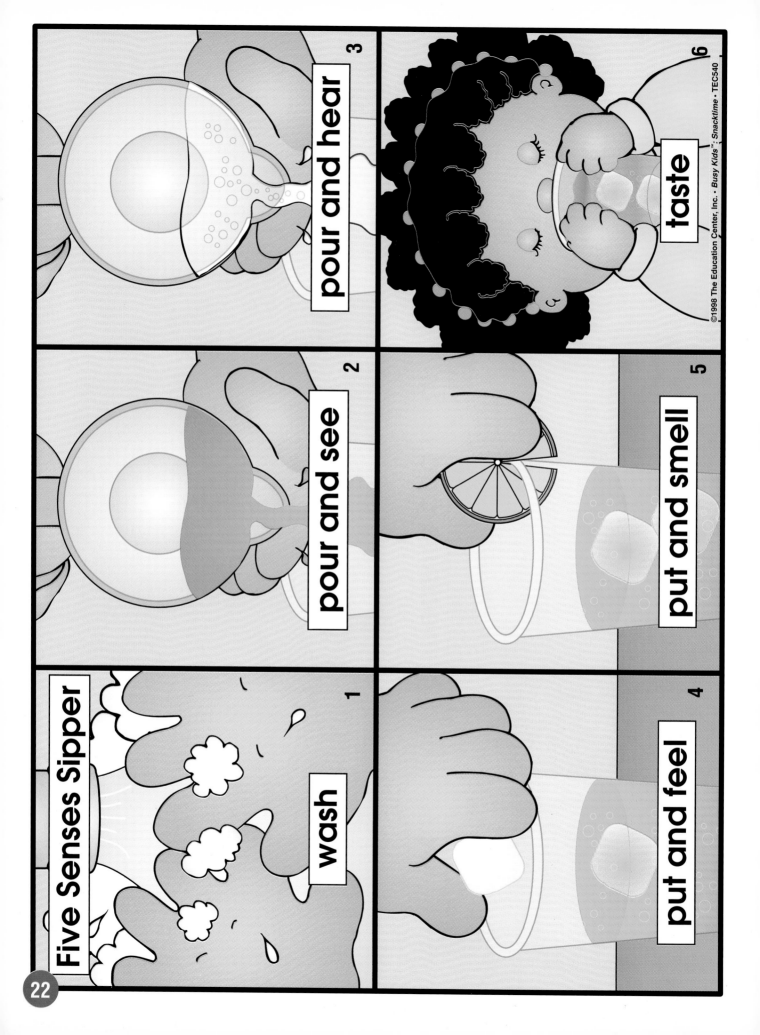

Five Senses Sipper

wash **1**

pour and see **2**

pour and hear **3**

put and feel **4**

put and smell **5**

taste **6**

©1998 The Education Center, Inc. • *Busy Kids*™: *Snacktime* • TEC540

The Five Senses

Five Senses Sipper

Ingredients:
approximately 1/2 cup orange juice per child
approximately 1/4 cup seltzer per child
2 ice cubes per child
1 orange slice per child

Utensils And Supplies:
one 8-ounce plastic cup per child
2 small pitchers
knife

Teacher Preparation:
Cut the oranges into slices. On each slice, cut along one section line from the rind to the center. Pour the orange juice and seltzer into separate pitchers.
Arrange the ingredients and utensils near the step-by-step direction cards.

What To Do When The Snack Is Through

Here is a "sense-ible" and scientific way to use your leftover ingredients. Put the following into three separate jars: 1/4 cup orange juice, 1/4 cup seltzer, and two ice cubes. Tightly fasten the lids; then display the jars in front of the class. How are the contents of the jars different? How are they the same? Shake each jar for several seconds; then ask youngsters to describe what they see and hear. Blindfold a student; then shake the jars again. Can she determine the contents of the jars by what she hears? Remove the lids. Can she guess the contents of the jars by what she smells?

Friends

Flavorful Friends

Ingredients:
2 vanilla or chocolate wafer cookies per child (purchase one package of each to allow for children's
choices)
10 pretzel sticks per child
red, brown, and yellow decorating gel

Utensils And Supplies:
napkins

Teacher Preparation:
Arrange the ingredients and utensils near the
step-by-step direction cards.

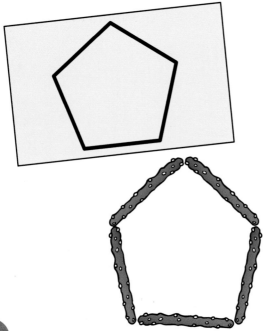

What To Do When The Snack Is Through
Use any leftover pretzels to help shape up math
skills. On separate index cards, draw a triangle, a
square, a rectangle, a pentagon, a hexagon, and an
octagon. Put the drawings and the extra pretzels at a
table. Then invite youngsters to use the pretzels to
copy the shapes on the cards.

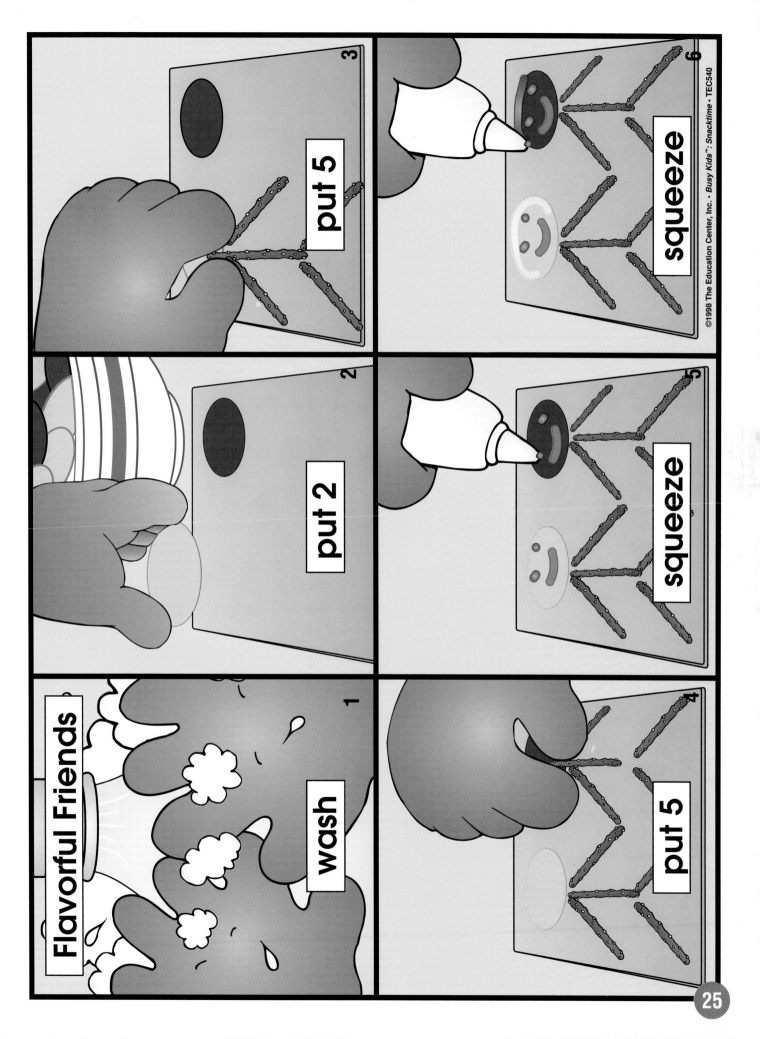

©1998 The Education Center, Inc. • Busy Kids™ • Snacktime • TEC540

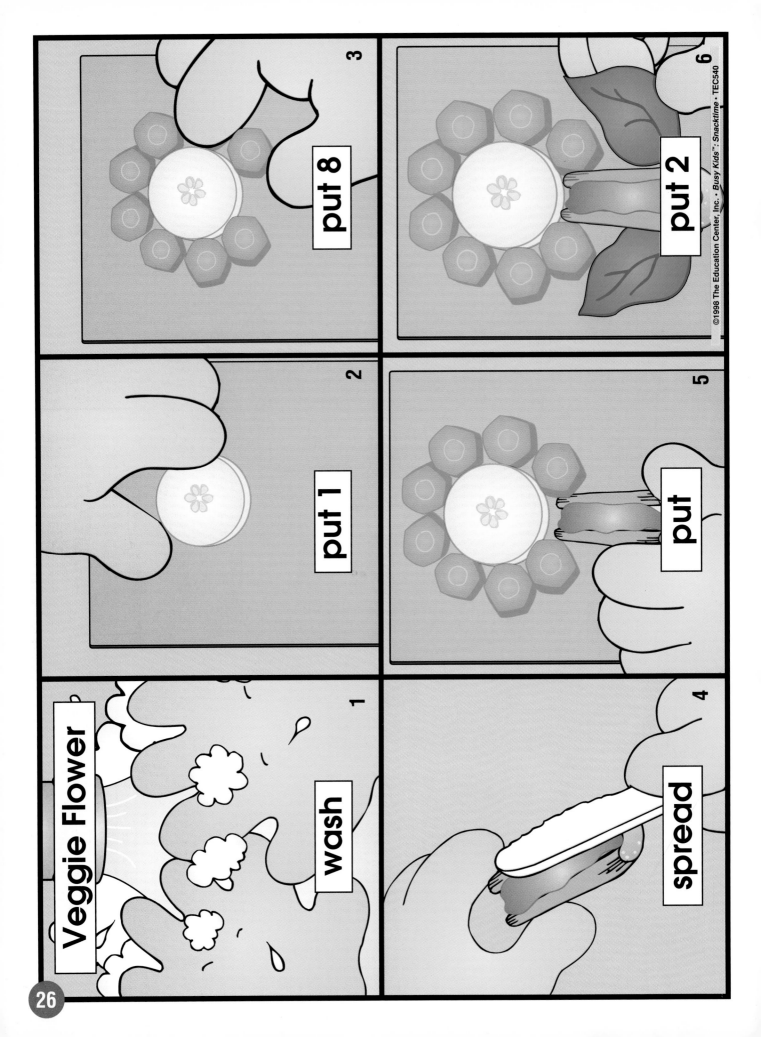

Veggie Flower

wash **1**

put 1 **2**

put 8 **3**

spread **4**

put **5**

put 2 **6**

©1998 The Education Center, Inc. • *Busy Kids*™: *Snacktime* • TEC540

Garden

Veggie Flower

Ingredients:
1 cucumber slice per child
8 carrot rounds per child
1/2 celery stalk per child
peanut butter
2 salad leaves (such as spinach) per child

Utensils And Supplies:
1 plastic knife (or craft stick) per child
napkins
vegetable peeler
knife

Teacher Preparation:
   Wash the celery stalks; then trim the ends and cut them in half. Peel and slice the necessary number of cucumbers and carrots. Wash the salad leaves. Arrange the ingredients and utensils near the step-by-step direction cards.

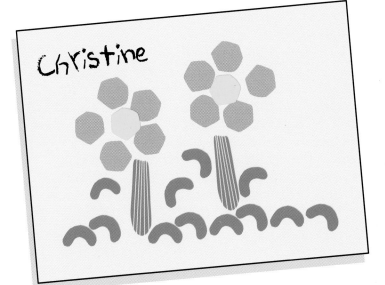

What To Do When The Snack Is Through

   Watch smiles blossom as your little sprouts use leftover celery and carrots to create garden paintings. Set out construction paper and a few colors of tempera paint. Invite each child to use the length of a celery stalk to print stems, and the end of a cut carrot to print flower centers and petals. Have her add leaves and grass by printing with the end of a celery stalk. Pretty!

Health & Safety

Stop 'n' Drop Roll

Ingredients:
1 slice of bread per child
peanut butter
jelly

Utensils And Supplies:
1 plastic knife (or craft stick) per child
napkins
2 spoons
knife

Teacher Preparation:
Trim the crusts from each slice of bread. Arrange the ingredients and utensils near the step-by-step direction cards.

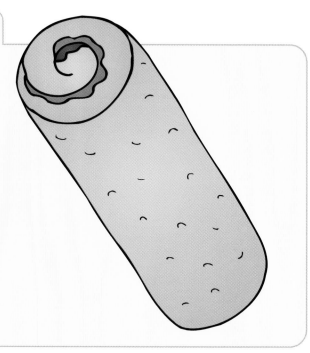

What To Do When The Snack Is Through

Stop! Don't throw away those bread crusts. Use them—and any leftover bread slices—to make some easy sculpting dough. Crumble up the crusts and slices into small pieces. Then mix in one teaspoon of glue for every one-fourth cup of crumbs. Give each child a small ball of the mixture to shape into a tiny pinch pot or other shape. Leave the sculptures to dry and harden overnight. If desired, decorate the dried projects with tempera paint.

©1998 The Education Center, Inc. • Busy Kids™: Snacktime • TEC540

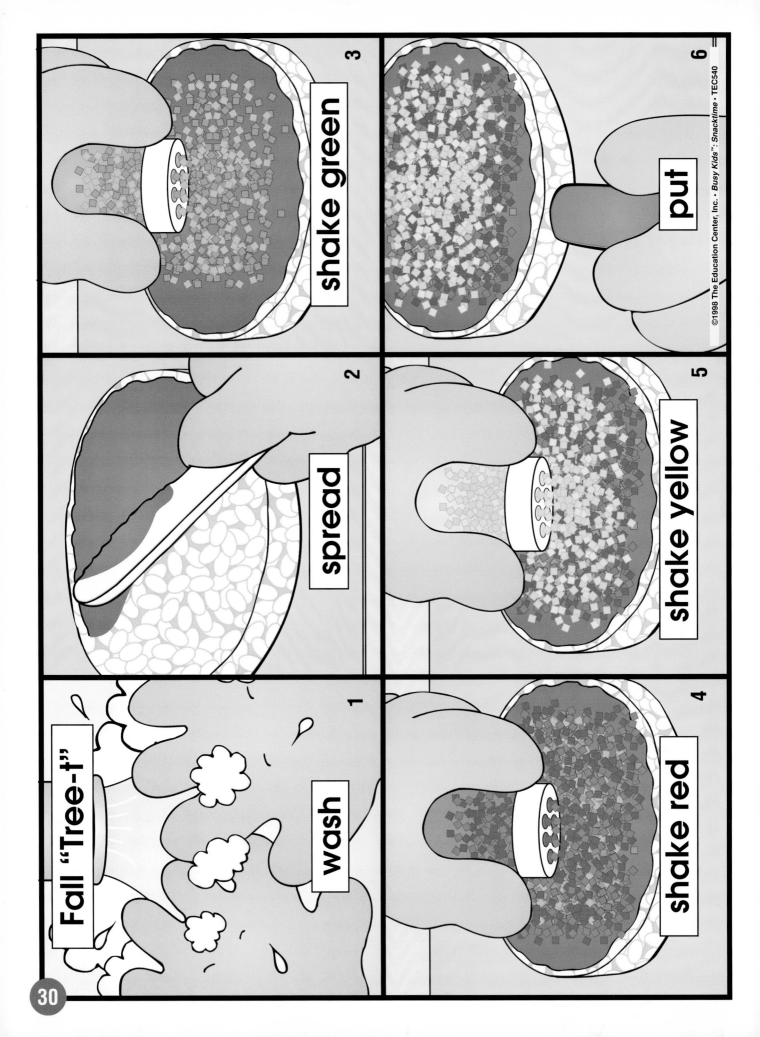

Fall "Tree-t"

wash 1

spread 2

shake green 3

shake red 4

shake yellow 5

put 6

©1998 The Education Center, Inc. • *Busy Kids*™: *Snacktime* • TEC540

Leaves

Fall "Tree-t"

Ingredients:
1 rice cake per child
1/4 carrot per child
peanut butter
Betty Crocker® Decor Selects sugar crystals in green,
    red, and yellow

Utensils And Supplies:
1 plastic knife (or craft stick) per child
napkins
vegetable peeler
knife

Teacher Preparation:
    Peel the necessary number of carrots; then cut off
the pointed tips. Cut each carrot in half; then slice
each piece in half lengthwise. Arrange the ingredients
and utensils near the step-by-step direction cards.

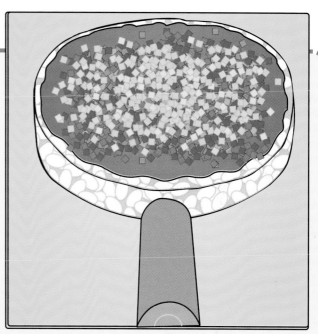

What To Do When The Snack Is Through

    Help size up your youngsters' math skills with the
help of any extra carrots. Cut each leftover carrot into
several carrot sticks of varied lengths; then put all the
sticks in a resealable plastic bag. Prepare a desired
number of plastic bags in the same manner; then put
the bags in a center. Invite little ones who visit the center to put the carrot sticks from a bag in order by size.

Moms And Dads

Sweet Treats

Ingredients:
2 Fig Newtons® (or any flavor Newtons®) per child
powdered sugar

Utensils And Supplies:
1 resealable plastic bag per child
spoon
knife

Note: If you plan to prepare the parent gift described in "What To Do When The Snack Is Through," you'll need to double the number of Fig Newtons® and plastic bags.

Teacher Preparation:
   Cut the two breaded edges off each cookie to reveal the filling; then cut each cookie into three rectangles. Arrange the ingredients and utensils near the step-by-step direction cards.

What To Do When The Snack Is Through
Have youngsters follow the direction cards again to make the same snack as a gift for their parents. Help each child wrap her cookies in a square sheet of plastic wrap and tie the bundle with curling ribbon. Attach a tag with a copy of the following poem:

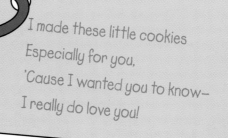

I made these little cookies
Especially for you,
'Cause I wanted you to know—
I really do love you!

©1998 The Education Center, Inc. • Busy Kids™: Snacktime • TEC540

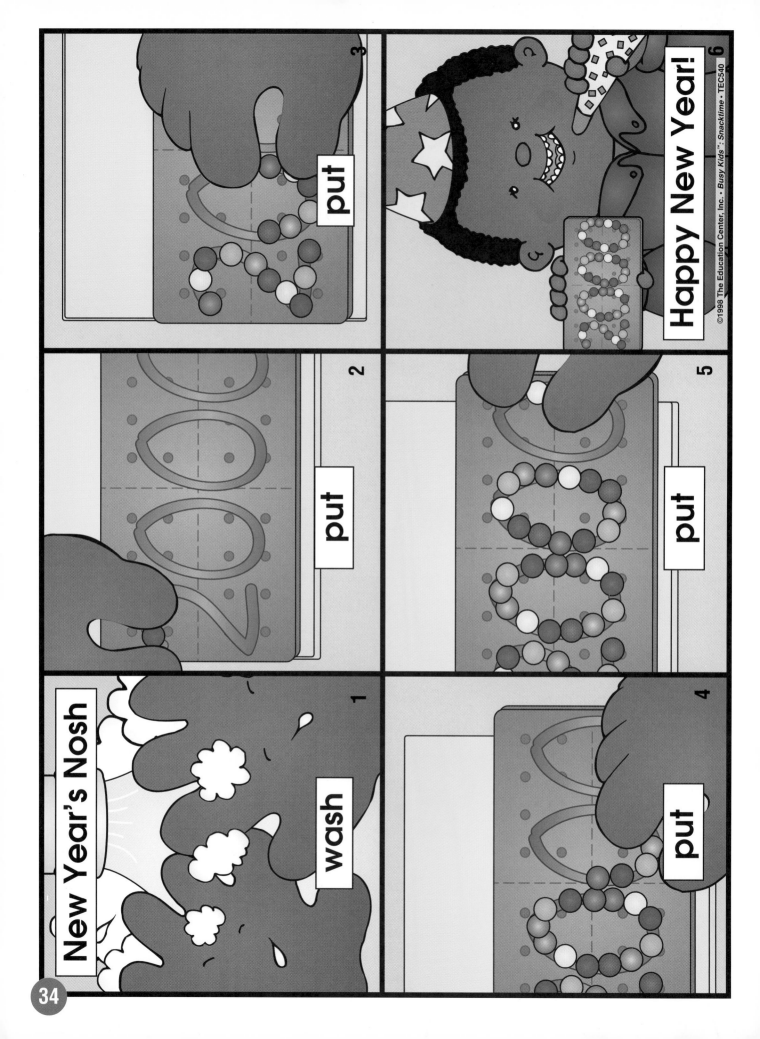

New Year

New Year's Nosh

Ingredients:
1 graham cracker per child
decorating gel (any color)
M&M's® Mini Baking Bits

Utensils And Supplies:
napkins

Teacher Preparation:
Use decorating gel to write the numerals for the New Year on each graham cracker. Arrange the ingredients and utensils near the step-by-step direction cards.

What To Do When The Snack Is Through

Bring in the New Year with a "lotto" fun! To make a lotto card, draw a grid on an index card and color the squares the same colors as the baking bits. (Repeat colors if necessary.) For older students, you may want to program the lotto cards with color words instead. Make a desired number of lotto cards with varied color (or color word) patterns. Place the cards and a plastic bag containing the leftover baking bits in a center. Invite small groups of youngsters to play lotto by matching the baking bits to the colors (or color words) on their lotto cards.

Nursery Rhymes

Hi, Humpty!

Ingredients:
1/2 hard-boiled egg per child
2 raisins per child
Hellmann's® Dijonnaise™
sweet relish
carrots

Utensils And Supplies:
1 plastic spoon per child
1 small paper cup per child
napkins
knife
vegetable peeler
grater
mixing bowl
tablespoon

Teacher Preparation:
   Hard-boil one egg for every two children; then remove the shells. Cut each egg in half lengthwise. For each child, put the yolk from an egg half into a separate plastic cup. Peel and grate a large carrot. For every six eggs (12 servings), combine a mixture of 1 tablespoon relish, 2 tablespoons Dijonnaise™, and 1 tablespoon grated carrots. Peel a second carrot and slice it into rounds; then cut each carrot round in half. Arrange the ingredients and utensils near the step-by-step direction cards.

What To Do When The Snack Is Through

   Use a leftover hard-boiled egg and a raw egg for an "eggs-traordinary" science experiment. Challenge youngsters to guess which egg is raw and which is cooked. Explain that you can tell the difference by spinning each egg. Tell students that if you stop each spinning egg with your finger, the hard-boiled egg will stop immediately, but the raw egg will keep moving a bit after you take your hand away. Try the experiment and ask youngsters to help you determine which egg is cooked and which is raw. Crack the eggs open to check.

   (What happened? The cooked egg reacts to the motion as a solid object. But the liquid inside the raw egg continues to shift from the spinning, causing enough force to keep the egg moving.)

©1998 The Education Center, Inc. • *Busy Kids™* • *Snacktime* • TEC540

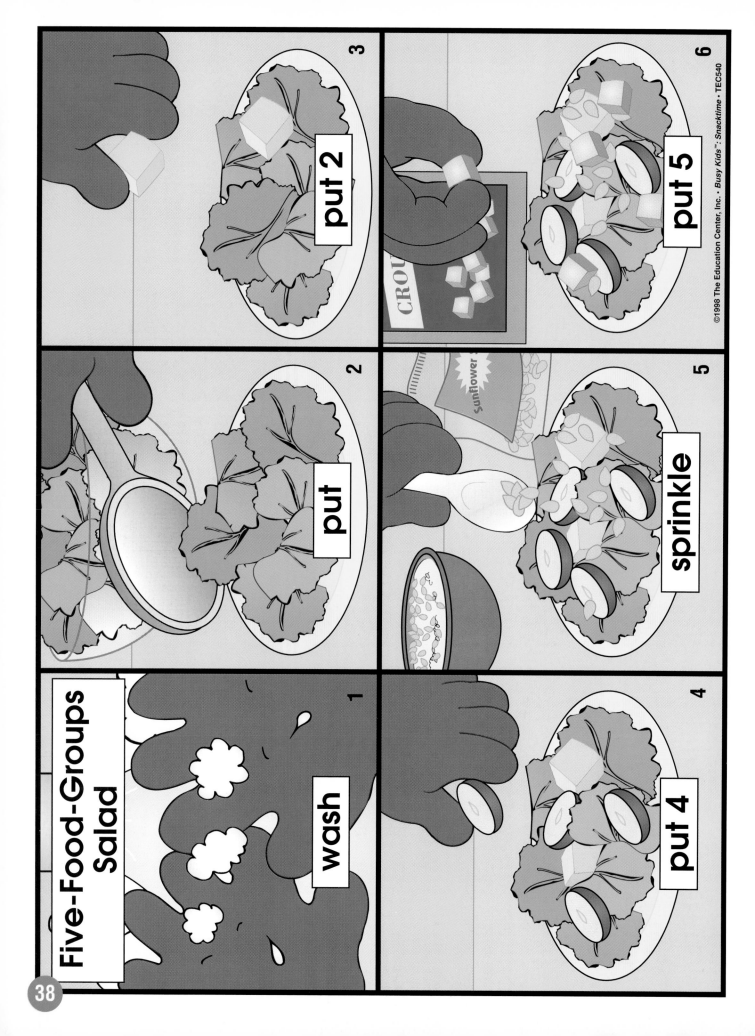

Five-Food-Groups Salad

1 wash

2 put

3 put 2

4 put 4

5 sprinkle

6 put 5

©1998 The Education Center, Inc. • Busy Kids™: Snacktime • TEC540

Nutrition

Five-Food-Groups Salad

Ingredients:
approximately 1/2 cup torn lettuce per child
2 cubes of cheese per child
4 grape halves per child
1 teaspoon sunflower seeds per child
5 croutons per child

Utensils And Supplies:
1 paper plate per child
1 plastic fork per child
1 large serving spoon
1 teaspoon
knife

Teacher Preparation:
   Wash and tear the lettuce into bite-size pieces. Cut the cheese into small cubes. Wash and slice the grapes. Arrange the ingredients and utensils near the step-by-step direction cards. If desired, have salad dressing available for those children who want it.

What To Do When The Snack Is Through
   This fine-motor activity stacks up to a lot of fun! Give each child a handful of croutons. Ask him to build a tall tower by stacking the croutons on top of one another. Once he is finished constructing, invite him to devour his tower!

Ocean

Sand Pail

Ingredients:
1/3 cup prepared instant vanilla pudding per child
3 vanilla wafers per child
string licorice
shell candy (optional)

Utensils And Supplies:
1 zippered plastic bag per child
one 5-oz. paper cup per child
1 plastic spoon per child

1/3-cup measuring cup
large mixing bowl
knife

Teacher Preparation:
   In a large bowl, make the pudding according to package directions. Punch two opposing holes at the top of each paper cup. Cut the string licorice so that you have a nine-inch length for each child. Arrange the ingredients and utensils near the step-by-step direction cards. If desired, purchase shell candy from a specialty candy store, and have students add a few pieces to their finished sand pails.

What To Do When The Snack Is Through

   Use extra vanilla pudding for pudding painting. Encourage each child to fingerpaint her name, shapes, or sea creatures. Make cookie crumbs from any leftover vanilla wafers; then place the crumbs on a cookie sheet. As each child finishes painting, encourage her to press her pudding-covered hands in the cookie crumbs to make her hands "sandy." Then invite her to lick the sand right off her hands. Mmm, tasty!

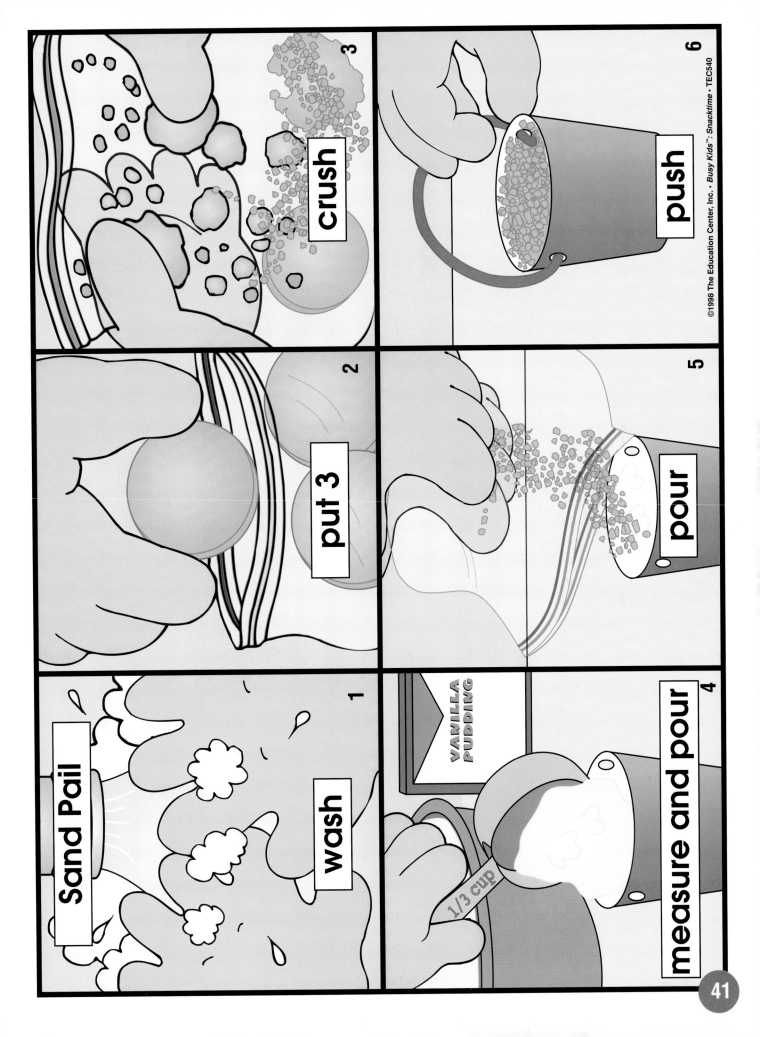

crush

push

put 3

pour

wash

Sand Pail

VANILLA PUDDING

measure and pour

1/3 cup

©1998 The Education Center, Inc. • *Busy Kids™: Snacktime* • TEC540

41

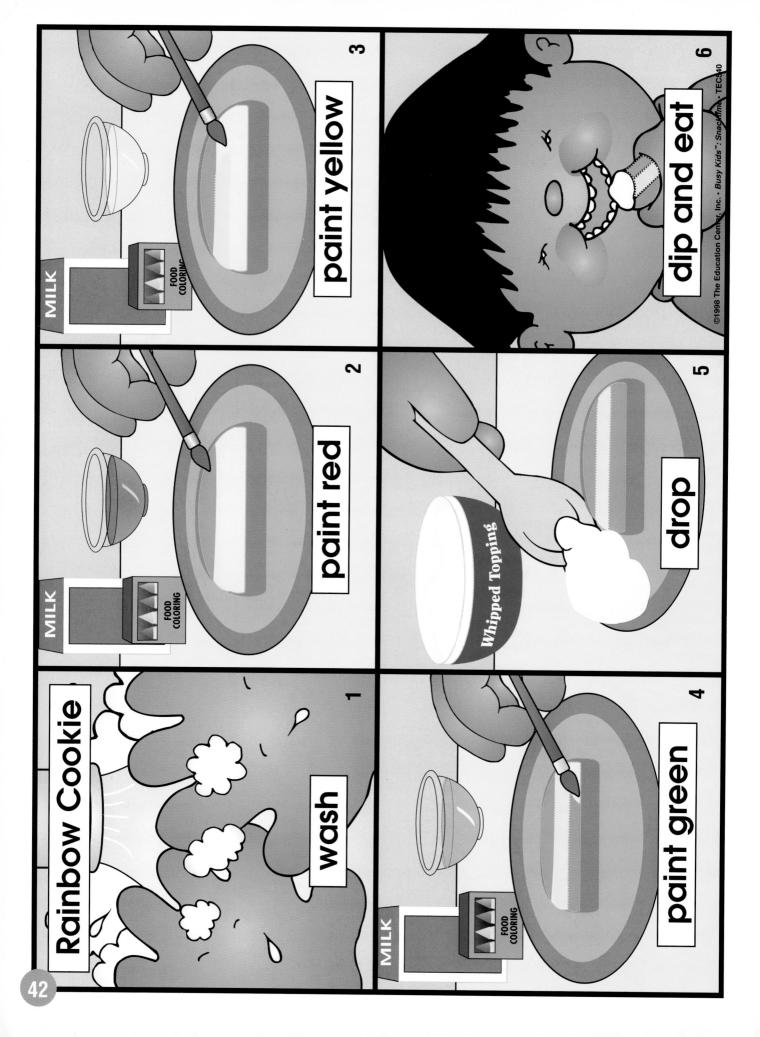

Rainbow Cookie

wash 1

paint red 2

paint yellow 3

paint green 4

drop 5

dip and eat 6

MILK

FOOD COLORING

Whipped Topping

©1998 The Education Center, Inc. • Busy Kids™: Snacktime • TEC840

Rain

Rainbow Cookie

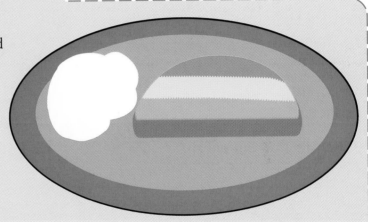

Ingredients:
1 Stella D'oro® Anisette Sponge® cookie per child
whipped topping
food coloring
1 1/2 cups milk

Utensils And Supplies:
1 small paper plate per child
3 plastic bowls
new, thin paintbrushes
spoon

Teacher Preparation:
   Pour a half cup of milk into each of three plastic
bowls. Use food coloring to tint one bowl of milk red,
one yellow, and one green. Put a new, thin paintbrush
in each container of milk. Arrange the ingredients and
utensils near the step-by-step direction cards.

What To Do When
The Snack Is Through
   Give each youngster a dollop of whipped topping
on a paper plate and invite him to mix a drop of food
coloring into the topping with his fingers. Encourage
him to add a drop of a different color to the whipped
topping and mix it in. What new color has he created?
When he is through experimenting with the colors,
invite him to lick his fingers clean!

Rocks, Dirt, And Mud

Mud To Munch

Ingredients:
1 tablespoon instant chocolate pudding mix per child
1/4 cup milk per child
Cocoa Puffs® cereal
minimarshmallows

Utensils And Supplies:
one 5-oz. plastic cup per child
1 plastic spoon per child
tablespoon
1/4-cup measuring cup

Teacher Preparation:
  Arrange the ingredients and utensils near the step-by-step direction cards.

What To Do When The Snack Is Through

  Use the leftover marshmallows and Cocoa Puffs® cereal for a bit of hands-on math practice. Cut an abstract shape from brown construction paper for each child in a small group. Have each child in a group take a paper "mud puddle" and a supply of "white rocks" (marshmallows) and "brown rocks" (cereal pieces). Have the children count and follow directions as you present math challenges, such as, "Put six brown rocks in your mud puddle. Add two white rocks to your puddle. How many rocks are in the puddle now?"

Mud To Munch

1 — wash

2 — measure and put
CHOCOLATE PUDDING
TBSP

3 — pour
1/4 cup

4 — stir

5 — put rocks
Puffs
Mini Marshmallows

6 — munch mud

©1998 The Education Center, Inc. • Busy Kids™ • Snacktime • TEC540

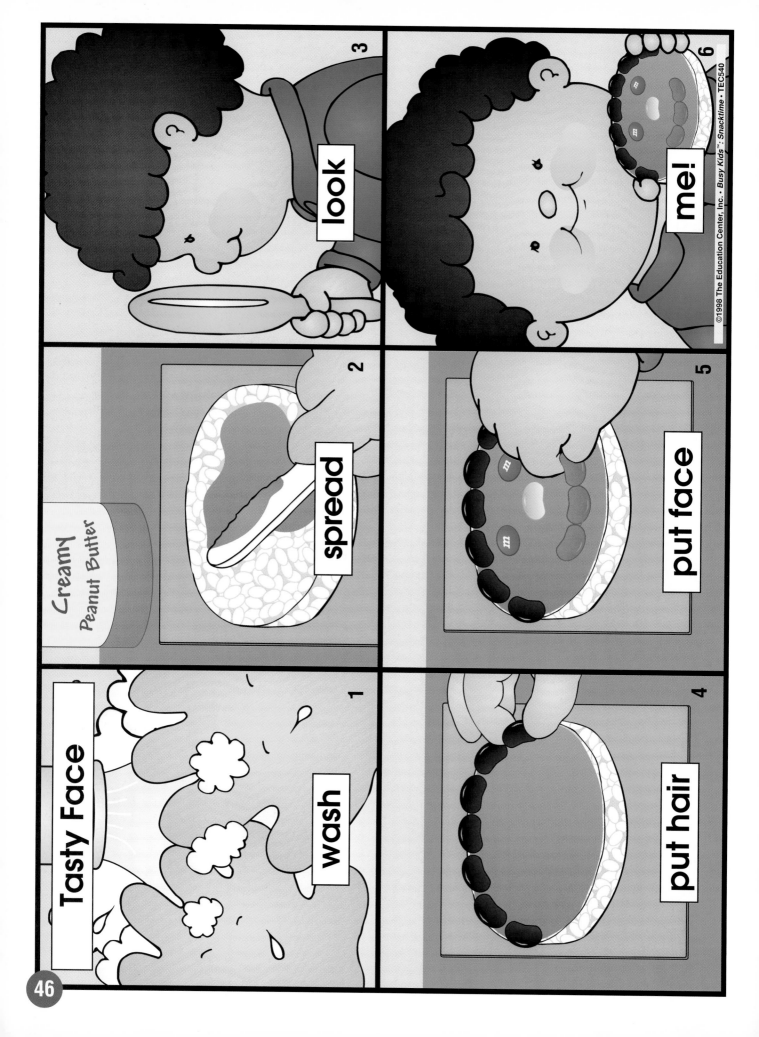

Tasty Face

Creamy Peanut Butter

wash **1**

spread **2**

look **3**

put hair **4**

put face **5**

me! **6**

©1998 The Education Center, Inc. • Busy Kids™ : Snacktime • TEC540

Self-Awareness

Tasty Face

Ingredients:
1 rice cake per child
creamy peanut butter
jelly beans
M&M's® candies

Utensils And Supplies:
1 plastic knife (or craft stick) per child
napkins
mirror

Teacher Preparation:
Arrange the ingredients and utensils near the step-by-step direction cards. Explain to youngsters that each of them should use candies that match his or her own hair color and eye color.

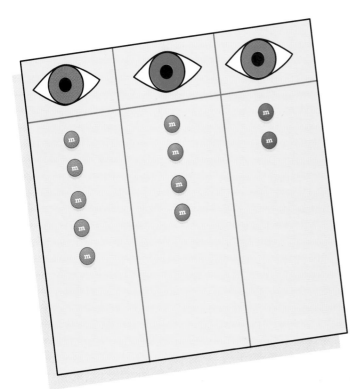

What To Do When The Snack Is Through

Use your extra M&M's® for a graphing lesson on your students' favorite subject—themselves! Make a simple bar graph with three columns. Draw an eye at the top of each column; then color one eye brown, one blue, and one green. Have each youngster use a mirror to identify his own eye color. Then have him locate an M&M's® candy that is the same color as his eyes. Have him use a glue stick to glue it to the appropriate column on the bar graph. When the graph is complete, have youngsters eye the graph and discuss the results.

Shadows

Shadows

Saucy Shadow

Ingredients:
1/2 English muffin per child
pizza sauce
1 slice of white cheese per child
1/2 slice of turkey luncheon meat per child

Utensils And Supplies:

knife	spoon
aluminum foil	small gingerbread-person cookie cutter
waxed paper	1 small paper plate per child (for serving)

Teacher Preparation:
   Cut the necessary number of English muffins in half. Cut each slice of luncheon meat in half. Tear or cut a foil square and a waxed-paper square for each child. Arrange the ingredients and utensils near the step-by-step direction cards. Be prepared to supervise the toasting of the snacks.

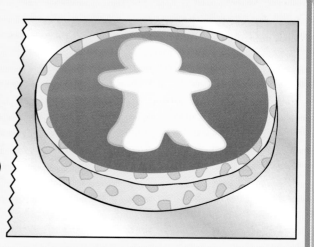

What To Do When The Snack Is Through

   Invite your youngsters to sink their teeth into this meaty math activity that reinforces patterning. Cut or tear the scraps from the meat and cheese slices into pieces. Give each child a napkin. Encourage him to lay out a pattern with the meat and cheese pieces, then eat up as he "reads" his pattern aloud. Mmm...turkey, cheese, turkey, cheese...

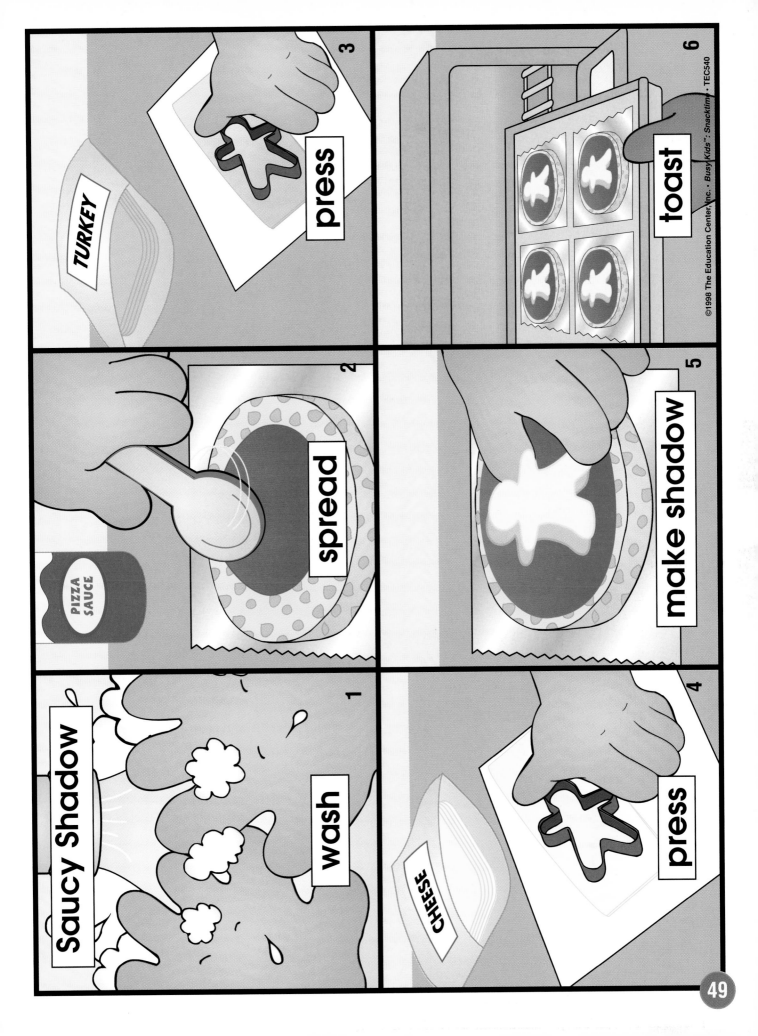

©1998 The Education Center, Inc. • *BusyKids™: Snacktime* • TEC540

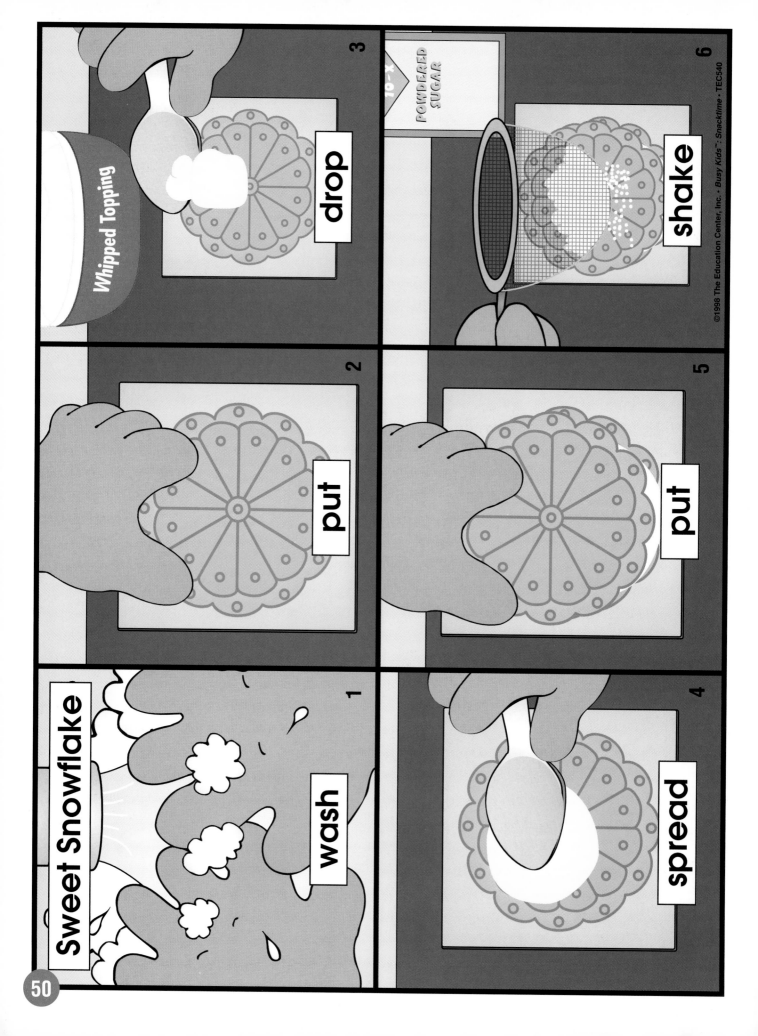

Sweet Snowflake

wash 1

put 2

drop 3
Whipped Topping

spread 4

put 5

shake 6
POWDERED SUGAR
10-X

©1998 The Education Center, Inc. • *Busy Kids*™: *Snacktime* • TEC540

50

SNOW

Sweet Snowflake

Ingredients:
2 Pizzelle Italian-style cookies per child
whipped topping
powdered sugar

Utensils And Supplies:
napkins
spoon
small sieve

Teacher Preparation:
   Arrange the ingredients and utensils near the step-by-step direction cards.

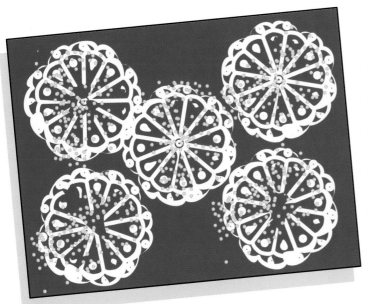

What To Do When The Snack Is Through

   Use some leftover Pizzelle cookies to make shimmering snowflake prints. Provide blue construction paper, silver glitter, and a shallow container of white tempera paint. Encourage each youngster to dip a cookie into the paint and then press it onto his paper. Then have him shake silver glitter onto the wet paint.

   As a variation, mix some dish detergent into the white paint; then make some Pizzelle prints on your classroom windows to give your classroom a frosty glow!

51

Space

Space Snack

Ingredients:
1 graham cracker per child
chocolate frosting
1 Danish wedding cookie per child
star-shaped decorating sprinkles

Utensils And Supplies:
1 plastic knife (or craft stick) per child
napkins

Teacher Preparation:
   Arrange the ingredients and utensils near the step-by-step direction cards.

What To Do When The Snack Is Through

   Your little space explorers will enjoy this star-studded activity. Direct youngsters to scatter around your classroom, pretending to be stars in the sky. Then use clear tape to attach a leftover star-shaped decorating sprinkle to the back of each child's hand. At a given signal, have your little stars search the sky for other stars of the same color. Once two children with the same-colored stars find one another, have them hold hands while searching for more stars. Continue until every star has joined his color constellation.

©1998 The Education Center, Inc. • Busy Kids™ • Snacktime • TEC540

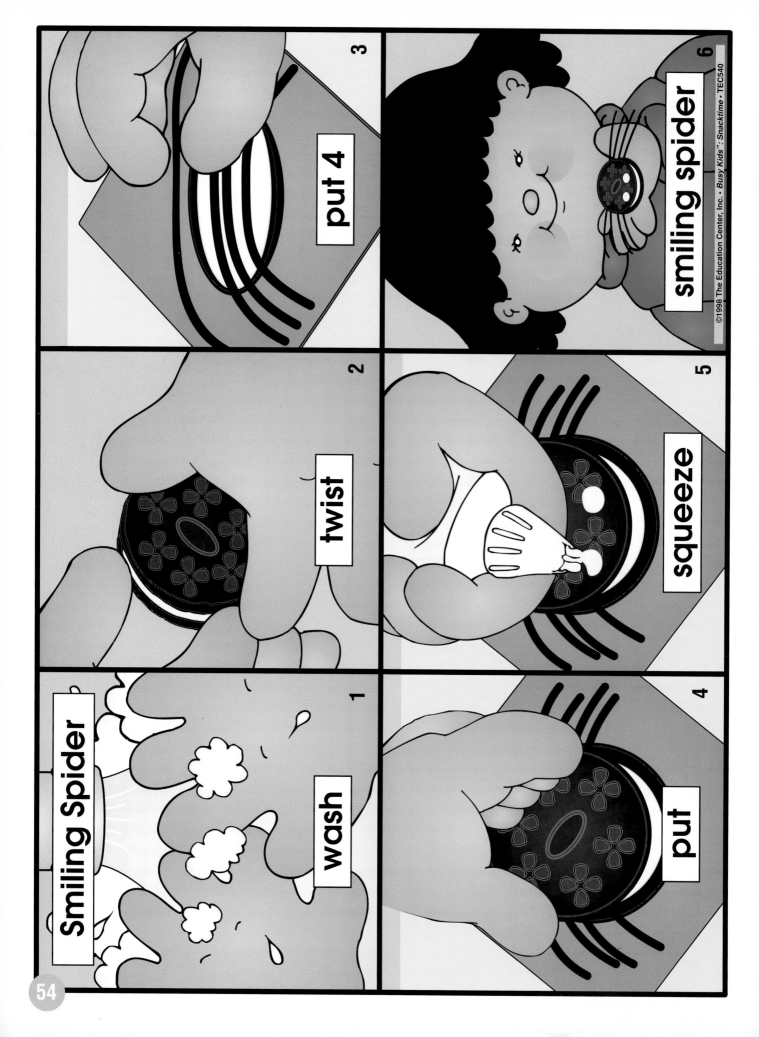

3 | put 4

6 | smiling spider
©1998 The Education Center, Inc. • *Busy Kids™ : Snacktime* • TEC540

2 | twist

5 | squeeze

1 | Smiling Spider | wash

4 | put

Spiders And Bats

Smiling Spider

Ingredients:
1 Oreo® cookie per child
4 five-inch lengths of black string licorice per child
tube of white decorating icing

Utensils And Supplies:
napkins

Teacher Preparation:
Cut string licorice into five-inch lengths. Gently twist the top and bottom of each cookie to loosen it. Arrange the ingredients and utensils near the step-by-step direction cards.

What To Do When The Snack Is Through
Little ones love to twist open Oreo® cookies to get to the cream filling. And it's a fun way to strengthen fine-motor skills! At another snacktime, give each child two cookies on which to practice his twisting talent. If he breaks a cookie, encourage him to design a cookie creature using the broken pieces and leftover decorating icing. Serve some milk to help wash down these cookie creatures.

Thanksgiving

Gobble! Gobble!

Ingredients:
1 large round cookie per child
1 chocolate Nutter Butter® cookie per child
3 candy corns per child
2 peanut-butter chips per child
tube of red decorating gel
6 pretzel sticks per child

Utensils And Supplies:
napkins

Teacher Preparation:
Arrange the ingredients and utensils near the step-by-step direction cards.

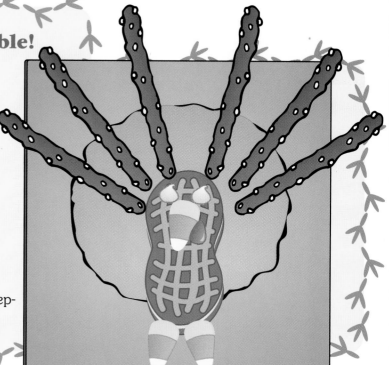

What To Do When The Snack Is Through

Here's a letter-formation activity your youngsters will stick with! Write the following uppercase letters on lined chart paper: *A, E, F, H, I, K, L, M, N, T, V, W, X, Y, Z.* (Make each letter two lines tall.) Place the chart paper on a table along with any extra pretzel sticks. Invite your little ones to form each letter by placing the pretzel sticks on top of the letters on the chart paper. For older students, display the chart paper in a prominent place, and encourage the children to use the pretzel sticks to form the letters on a tabletop.

©1998 The Education Center, Inc. • Busy Kids™: Snacktime • TEC540

"Chew-Chew" Train

1 wash

2 put 2

3 put 4

4 put

5 push in

6 put 5

©1998 The Education Center, Inc. • *Busy Kids*™: *Snacktime* • TEC540

Transportation

"Chew-Chew" Train

Ingredients:
1 chocolate-covered cake roll per child
Oreo O's™ cereal

Utensils And Supplies:
3 coffee stirrers per child
napkins

Teacher Preparation:
   Arrange the ingredients and utensils near the step-by-step direction cards.

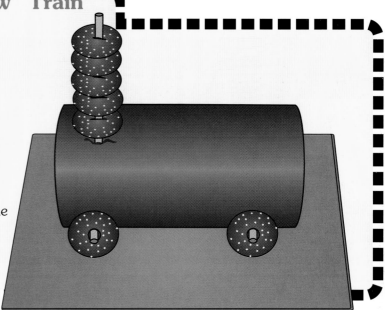

What To Do When The Snack Is Through

   Use the leftover cereal pieces and some more coffee stirrers to give youngsters practice with estimation. Provide each child with a coffee stirrer, a bit of play dough, and a handful of Oreo O's™ cereal. Have him stick his blob of play dough on a tabletop, then push his coffee stirrer into the play dough so that it stands upright. Then ask him to estimate how many cereal pieces will fit on the coffee stirrer. Can he fit ten? More than ten? Have him stack the cereal pieces on his coffee stirrer to find the answer.

Valentine's Day

Love Bug

Ingredients:
1 red Jell-O® Jigglers™ heart shape per child
2 candy conversation hearts per child
1 slice of kiwi per child
red string licorice

Utensils And Supplies:
1 small paper plate per child
knife
spatula
heart-shaped cookie cutter

Teacher Preparation:
   Follow the package directions to make a batch of Jell-O® Jigglers™. Use a small heart-shaped cookie cutter to cut one heart from the gelatin for each child. Peel the necessary number of kiwi and cut them into slices; then cut the slices in half. Cut the string licorice into three-inch strands. Arrange the ingredients and utensils near the step-by-step direction cards.

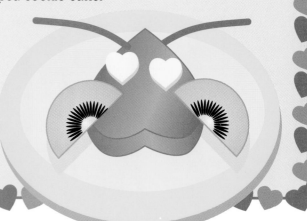

What To Do When The Snack Is Through

   Youngsters are bound to put their hearts into this prereading activity. Place your leftover candy conversation hearts on a tray. Be sure the words on each heart are showing. Then invite youngsters to match the candy hearts that bear the same sentiment. As a challenge for older students, read the sentiment on an unidentified heart. Then see if your youngsters can locate the heart that you quoted.

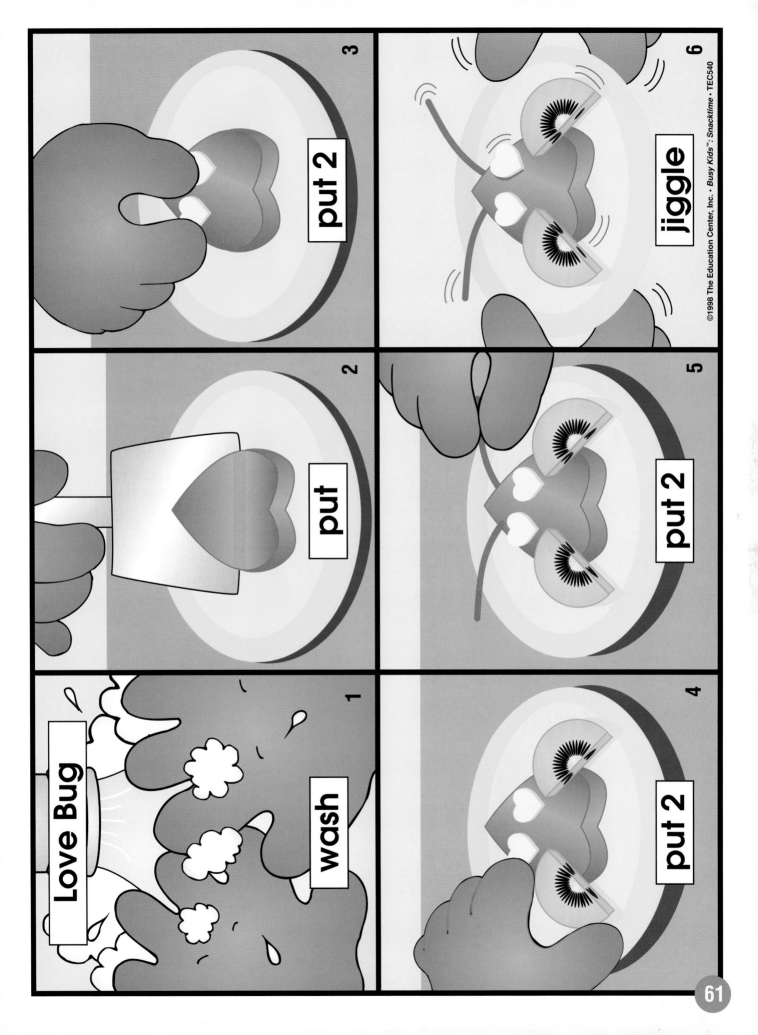

©1998 The Education Center, Inc. • Busy Kids™: Snacktime • TEC540

put bear food

3

feeding time

6

©1998 The Education Center, Inc. • Busy Kids™: Snacktime • TEC540

put monkey food

2

Banana Chips

put bird food

5

Sunflower Seeds

Zoo Food

wash

1

put crocodile food

4

Goldfish® Crackers

62

ZOO FOOD

Ingredients:
1 flat-bottomed ice-cream cone per child
dried banana chips
Craisins™ dried cranberries
Goldfish® crackers
sunflower seeds

Utensils And Supplies:
4 large spoons
knife

Teacher Preparation:
  Cut the dried banana chips into smaller pieces. Arrange the ingredients and utensils near the step-by-step direction cards.

WHAT TO DO WHEN
THE SNACK IS THROUGH

  What sort of fun can you have with leftover zoo food? Sorting fun! Pour any extra banana chips, Craisins™ dried cranberries, Goldfish® crackers, and sunflower seeds into one large bowl. Invite each child to spoon some of the mixture onto a napkin. Ask him to group all the same foods together. Ask questions to help youngsters compare the number of items in each group, using words such as *most, fewest,* and *equal.*

Dear Family,

We're very busy learning about _____.
(theme)

For our cooking activity, we plan to prepare _____.
(name of recipe)

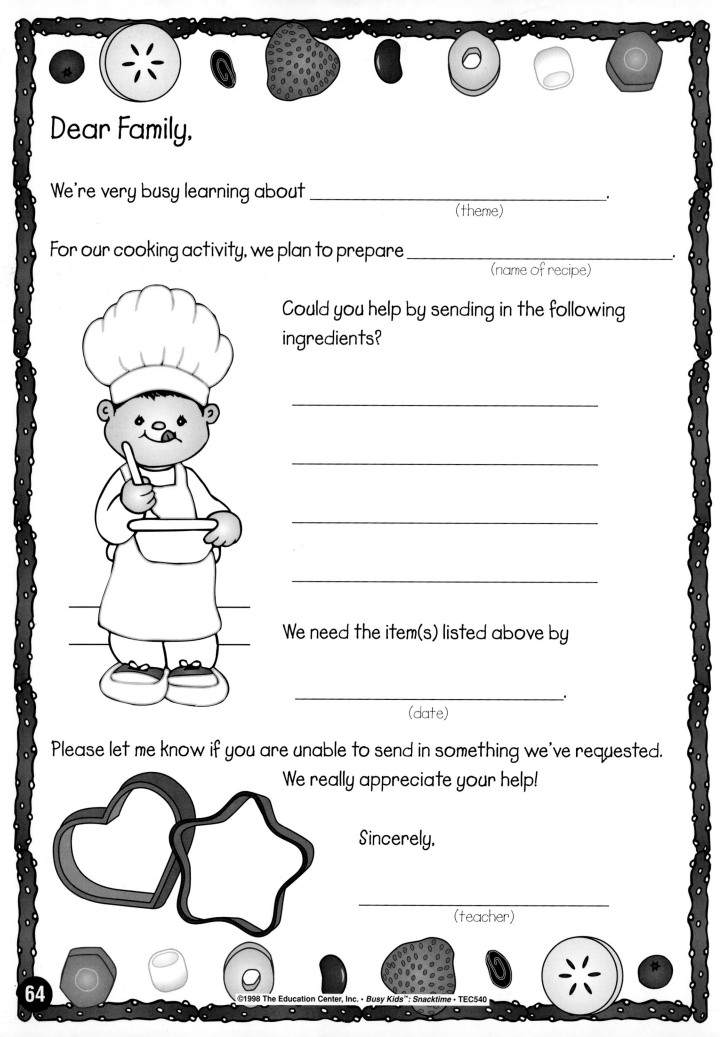

Could you help by sending in the following ingredients?

_____

_____

_____

_____

We need the item(s) listed above by

_____.
(date)

Please let me know if you are unable to send in something we've requested. We really appreciate your help!

Sincerely,

_____
(teacher)

©1998 The Education Center, Inc. • Busy Kids™: Snacktime • TEC540